CODE ACADEMY

and the

Code Confusion!

By Kirsty Holmes

BookLife
PUBLISHING

©2019
BookLife Publishing Ltd.
King's Lynn
Norfolk PE30 4LS

A catalogue record for this
book is available from the
British Library.

ISBN: 978-1-78637-555-1

Written by:
Kirsty Holmes

Edited by:
Emilie Dufresne

Designed by:
Drue Rintoul

All facts, statistics, web addresses and URLs in this book were verified as valid and accurate at time of writing. No responsibility for any changes to external websites or references can be accepted by either the author or publisher.

Some lines of code used in this book have been constructed for comedic purposes, and are not intended to represent working code.

IMAGE CREDITS

CONTENTS

Words that look like **this** can be found in the glossary on page 24.

REGISTRATION

Another day at Code Academy has begun.
Time for the register! Meet Class 101…

Ashwin
Subject: Programming

Frankie
Subject: Debugging

Jia
Subject: Hacking

Bailey
Subject: Memory

Simon
Subject: Coding

Sophia
Subject: Logic

Today's lesson is all about coding. We'll be finding out:

Ro-Bud

Subject: **Playtime!**

- What are computer languages?

- What is a compiler?

- What is machine code?

- What is binary code?

Code Academy is a school especially for kids who love computers... and robots too! Do I hear the bell...?

MORNING LESSON

The pupils at Code Academy are very excited. They are getting a new classmate today – a very special pupil indeed.

This is Ro-Bud! She's their new classmate, and she's going to help the pupils learn more about **artificial intelligence**.

Bonjour

Welcome

Hello

Hola

Namaste

Bienvenue

Say hello to Ro-Bud, everybody!

LUNCHTIME!

At lunchtime, the class are playing hopscotch outside.

One, two, three, four, five, six, seven, eight, nine!

Ro-Bud is watching and not joining in. It's hard being the new robot in school. Maybe she is feeling shy? The class try and invite her to play.

01101000
01100101
01101100
01110000

Sophia Says:

Why is Ro-Bud speaking in all those weird numbers? Ro-Bud - are you OK?

AFTERNOON LESSON

The class take Ro-Bud to Professor Chip straight away.

Ro-Bud can only understand the numbers 0 and 1, and the children can only understand words. How will they ever make friends?

Professor Chip takes the class to the whiteboard to discuss the problem.

We need to help Ro-Bud understand us. To do this, we need to think about computer languages.

BINARY CODE

1 0 ? 1 0 ?
0 1 ? 0 1 ?
1 0 ? 1 0 ?

Humans don't all speak one language – there are many languages we might use. For example, Sophia speaks Polish at home with her parents, but English here at school.

SIMON SORTS IT OUT

I don't speak Polish. So if I want to understand what Sophia said, I need to change the words she uses into words I understand. This is called translating.

I find the word I need in Polish, then look it up and the translator tells me the word I know in English. I can do this the other way too – from English into Polish – so I can answer!

Cześć!

TRANSLATOR

Hi!

It's the same with computers. Computers use a low-level language called binary to understand things. They **receive** this as a series of 0 and 1 digits. That's the language that Ro-Bud understands.

1001000 1001001
00100001

Humans can understand binary code, but it would take a long, long time to figure it all out. When we talk to computers, we need to use a high-level language that uses words, such as...

PYTHON ?
JAVASCRIPT ?
LISP ?
HTML
CSS

HASKELL ?
SCRATCH ?
RUBY ?
C++
XML

Jia's Ideas:

There are lots of languages to choose from!

CRACK THE CODE

When I go to Sophia's house for tea, I use a translator to help me talk to her parents. Sophia's mum has an **app** on her phone that we use.

So that Ro-Bud can understand us, and we can understand her, we need a translator. For computers, this is a piece of **software** called a compiler. I'll **install** it for Ro-Bud now.

Binary code uses numbers to **represent** letters. The compiler can take the high-level language in words, and very quickly turn it into binary code that Ro-Bud can understand.

HELLO!

COMPILER

01001000 01000101 01001100 01001100 01001111 00100001

ALL SORTED

Ro-Bud's new compiler means she can now understand the class – and she speaks so many languages that she can make friends with everyone!

Bonjour
0 1

Hello
1

Welcome
0 1

Hola
1

Bienvenue
1 0

Namaste
0

HOMEWORK

Can you write your name in binary code? What about a message to your friends? Remember that each group of eight digits will make one letter.

A	01000001	**J**	01001010	**S**	01010011
B	01000010	**K**	01001011	**T**	01010100
C	01000011	**L**	01001100	**U**	01010101
D	01000100	**M**	01001101	**V**	01010110
E	01000101	**N**	01001110	**W**	01010111
F	01000110	**O**	01001111	**X**	01011000
G	01000111	**P**	01010000	**Y**	01011001
H	01001000	**Q**	01010001	**Z**	01011010
I	01001001	**R**	01010010		

LOOK IT UP

GLOSSARY:

APP — short for application; a computer program, particularly for phones and tablets

ARTIFICIAL INTELLIGENCE — computers that can use reason and make decisions of their own

DICTIONARY — a book of words and their meanings, pronunciation and translations

INSTALL — put into position ready to use

PROGRAM — instructions that tell a computer what to do

RECEIVE — to get, take or experience

REPRESENT — to stand for something else

SOFTWARE — programs written to operate a computer

INDEX: